Trading Places in Timbuktu

A Tale From Mali

By Joyce A. Barnes
Illustrated by José Miralles

CELEBRATION
Pearson Learning Group

D1293208

Contents

The Trouble With Bela

Long ago, in the city of Timbuktu, Mali, there lived two boys. The one named Ismail— the son of a revered griot, or oral historian— was born into power and luxury. He lived in the palace compound, wore finely woven robes, and slept on soft cushions every night. His life was prosperous, and yet he was unsatisfied.

The other boy, Ahmadou, belonged to a family of nomadic traders. They had a difficult life, spent traveling over the Sahara Desert. Oddly enough, both Ahmadou and Ismail longed to travel a different road than the one we find them on as this tale begins.

"Get up, Bela!" Ahmadou cried at the stubborn camel parked in the middle of the busy Timbuktu marketplace.

"Yaaawwl," roared the old dromedary. The camel remained on the ground, her long, spindly legs tucked beneath her.

"If you want to eat, you'd better follow me. Your meal and bed lie at the end of this road, and I can't go to mine until you go to yours!"

Busy arguing with his camel, Ahmadou did not notice a boy about his own age who was standing and watching them.

"May I help?" the boy asked.

Ahmadou noticed the boy's crisp white robe. "What do you know about camels?"

4

"Not much, but I have ridden horses."

Ahmadou shrugged. "So what? A horse will listen to reason. A camel will listen to no one but itself. Get up, Bela!"

The camel blinked her long lashes and slowly chewed her cud. The boy in the white robe took a stand in front of Bela. While she was lying down, Bela's nose was level with his. "I command you to rise!" he shouted.

Bela cried, "Yaaawwl!" and spit on the startled boy.

"Ugh!" cried the boy.

"A camel's breath is so strong, you can tell one is approaching you from 20 steps behind!" Ahmadou said, laughing.

As the other boy took a finely woven cloth from his bag, Ahmadou stopped laughing. "Who are you, anyway?" he asked.

"I am Prince Ismail of Mali," Ismail said, wiping his face. "My uncle is the king."

Ahmadou fell to his knees. He had made fun of a prince! There was sure to be trouble.

"Excuse me, son of Mali," he apologized. "I thought you were a regular boy like me."

"I am!" said Ismail, helping Ahmadou up. "At least, I want to be. Please tell me your name and why you are wearing blue cloth."

Ahmadou looked down at his worn robe, the months of desert sand in its folds. "I am Ahmadou, son of Ibrahim and Jamilla," he said with pride. "We are caravan traders."

"You mean you have crossed the golden sands?" asked Ismail.

"Many times," Ahmadou said. "Well, three times, but I am young. We returned two days ago from a sixty-day trip. Father let me ride the lead camel, Bela. Now the camel refuses to go another step. Get up, Bela!"

With each sentence, Ismail's excitement grew. He spent his days reading about journeys. The more he read, the more he wanted to experience such a journey himself.

"You are lucky. I would give up all my manuscripts if I could trade places with you."

Ahmadou shook his head. "Being a caravan trader is very difficult."

"That may be, but you have seen so many wonderful things!"

Ahmadou looked again at Ismail's bag.

"I would gladly trade the heat, the thirst, the hard work, and the constant moving from place to place, if I could read even one of those books you have in your bag."

"Let's trade places!" said Ismail, his eyes flashing. "You and I are about the same age. We look enough alike. You put on my cap and gown, and I'll wrap my head in your blue veil. For one afternoon, I can pretend I am off on my next desert adventure, and you can have my manuscripts."

The offer tempted Ahmadou. He could read a little, and he had often wished to read a scholar's manuscript. Still, it was ridiculous to think he could change places with a prince.

"My clothes are dirty, and so am I. You don't want to change places with me."

Ismail didn't give up. "Come to the palace, and both you and your clothes can be washed. Then, we'll dress in each other's clothes and see if we can fool my brother.

Still Ahmadou refused.

"I'll read this manuscript to you," Ismail added, showing him the book, "and you can tell me all about crossing the desert. Then, we'll have supper with the other boys. It'll be fun!"

Ahmadou liked the thought of a meal at the palace, but a 1,300-pound obstacle stood, or rather sat, in his way. "I cannot leave Bela."

Ismail thought a moment and then dashed off. He returned quickly with a bucket of water and some grain. "Maybe this will revive Bela."

Ahmadou was impressed. This pampered son of Mali was a quick thinker, and he had enough money to feed someone else's camel. Maybe trading places with a prince wasn't a bad idea after all.

Bela liked the food and water, and she waited patiently as Ahmadou showed Ismail how to climb onto her saddle. Then, the camel rocked back and forth to stand. The boys rode Bela to the stables and secured the camel there.

"Now," said Ismail, "our adventure begins." They set off toward the palace.

Trading Places

The sun was setting behind a high, gold-tipped gate as the boys arrived. The palace compound lay in the Sankore quarter of Timbuktu. Spread out behind a mud brick wall, the compound held about 100 houses and stores, an inner and outer courtyard, and stables as finely built as the king's own abode.

"The boys' compound is this way," Ismail said, leading the way. "We are all young scholars."

They found Sudi pacing about. Before the servant could scold Ismail for running away from him in the marketplace, the prince commanded, "My friend Ahmadou is staying for supper. See that he gets a bath and that his clothes are cleaned and repaired." Sudi shook his head, as if wondering what the young prince was up to now, but he did what he was told.

While the boys waited for Sudi to bring the cleaned clothes, Ismail read to Ahmadou from the story of Sundiata, the Lion King of Mali. Ahmadou followed along with hungry eyes, wishing he, too, could understand all the marks on the page. Soon, Sudi returned with the freshly washed clothes. The boys shooed the suspicious servant away and then put their plan into action.

"I will change in Botu's room. You change in here." Ismail gave Ahmadou a new robe and a scholar's cap.

Ahmadou held onto his veil. He had only recently received it himself. To a nomad, a veil is a sign of honor. He stood uncertainly for what seemed like a long moment. Finally, with some trepidation, Ahmadou handed it to Ismail. The young prince rushed off to change.

When the two boys were dressed in each other's clothes, they stood before each other in amazement.

"In my scholar's cap and gown, you appear to look just like me!" Ismail said.

Ahmadou examined his friend. "We are two of a kind. Do you think we will fool anyone?"

"Come," Ismail urged. "Let's find out!"

They joined the other boys. Ismail's brother, Botu, sat at the head of the table. At 16, he was one of the leaders of the young men.

"Brothers and friends," he said. "This is the beginning of the end of my bachelorhood. Before a month has passed, I will wed Princess Amina of Songhai. Drink to my future!"

"Hurrah!" the others cheered as they swallowed gulps of goat's milk in Botu's honor.

Ismail and Ahmadou walked to the head of the table. "Ah, my youngest brother has finally arrived. Who is your blue-veiled friend, Ismail?"

"This is Ahmadou. He is a nomad," said Ahmadou.

Some of the boys whispered behind their hands, but Botu grabbed Ismail's hand and held it briefly. "Welcome, Ahmadou. Do not leave until you are full!"

Hiding a grin beneath the veil, Ismail replied, "Thank you, oh great son of Mali."

"You have soft hands for a nomad boy," Botu remarked.

Ismail drew his hand away. "I wear . . . camelskin coverings to protect them," he stammered.

Botu let the comment go. "Please sit. Eat!" He turned to Ahmadou and gave him a big hug. "Little brother, you have developed some muscles! Have you been secretly preparing to carry my bride to me at my wedding?"

Ahmadou cleared his throat and imitated Ismail's voice. "Yes, my brother. I lift stones every day."

"Good!" said Botu. "You must perform your duty well on my wedding day, or you doom our entire marriage."

Ahmadou nodded, though he had no idea what duty Botu referred to. *No matter*, he thought. *Tomorrow, I will be back with my family, tending the camels and wondering if this meeting with the king's nephews was a dream.*

The boys began eating. Ahmadou consumed all he could and then settled back to watch and listen as Botu discussed art and philosophy with the boys. He noticed that the princes carried themselves with confidence, and he began to imitate them. Meanwhile, Ismail entertained the younger boys with tales of desert adventures so great that Ahmadou started to believe the other boy was a nomad.

Back in Ismail's room, the two boys laughed until their stomachs ached. "My own brother did not even recognize me!" Ismail exclaimed.

"It was fun pretending to be a prince."

"Let's continue the game one more day."

This, of course, was Ismail's suggestion, but Ahmadou readily agreed.

"We must go to my family's tent now," Ahmadou said. "My mother may not be so easily fooled."

At dark, they reached the edge of the city. "We must hurry," Ahmadou said. "I—we—still have chores to do."

Ahmadou's family's tent was pitched in a clearing. "The first thing we must do is gather the goat herd and pen them for the night," Ahmadou explained. "Then, we must check the mules. I warn you: Being a nomad means doing a lot of work."

When the chores were done, the two exhausted boys crawled into the women's side of the tent. Jamilla, Ahmadou's mother, sat on a woven mat mixing millet flour and water in a bowl. "Why are you so late, Ahmadou?" she asked her son.

Ismail said, "Mother, I made a friend in the marketplace. This is Prince Ismail of Mali."

Jamilla looked up abruptly. She stood up and said, "Tiye! Kavitha! Bring us something to drink. There is a prince to see us!"

The two sisters brought cups of goat's milk into the tent. Kavitha whispered to Tiye, "He doesn't look like much of a prince. Where are his gold-tipped arrows?"

"I am a scholar," Ahmadou said, trying not to smile. "I study manuscripts, not warfare." The girls nodded, wide-eyed.

Jamilla smiled graciously. "Please sit down, Prince Ismail. Ahmadou, go to the other side of the tent and tell your father that you have brought a prince here tonight."

"Yes, Mother," said Ismail, with a quick glance at Ahmadou. He walked outside to the opposite end of the tent and stopped at the opening flap. How would he know Ahmadou's father, a man he had never seen?

"Who is outside the tent?" a muffled voice called from inside.

Ismail cleared his throat. "It is Ahmadou," he called, peeking inside the flap.

"Come in, my son!" The speaker, who was Ahmadou's father, Ibrahim, sat at the head of a group of blue-veiled men, all with glasses of brown tea in their hands.

"Here is Ahmadou," said Ibrahim proudly. "He earned his veil on our last trip. He managed all of my camels. Sit beside me, son."

Ismail beamed. He liked his "new" father right away. Sitting beside Ibrahim, Ismail forgot all about telling his father that the "prince" was on the other side of the tent.

The sun dropped behind the horizon. On the other side of the tent, Ahmadou told the story of Sundiata to his mother and two sisters, having memorized the tale after hearing it only once. Ahmadou's family never suspected that anything was wrong.

That night, the boys parted. "I will meet you after school tomorrow, outside of the great wall. Good luck, Ahmadou," Ismail said.

"Have fun working hard!" Ahmadou said with a laugh as he thought of the cushioned rest he would have that night.

"Wake up, Ahmadou!"

Ismail heard the command in his dream. "Just a bit longer, Sudi," Ismail said, not opening his eyes.

Ibrahim's voice rose. "Come with me to help hitch up the camels. We are leaving."

Ismail opened his eyes and saw the veiled man above him. He remembered the game.

"Yes, Father!" he said, hopping up immediately. Outside it was still dark, and Jamilla and Ahmadou's sisters were methodically placing items from the tent onto three mules.

"Where are we going, Mother?" Ismail called.

"We're going to Walata. A prime supply of salt awaits. If we can sell this, we may settle in Timbuktu next year. Hurry, you know your father is eager to be gone."

"Is Walata in the desert?" Ismail asked.

"You know that it is. It's ten days' travel from here. Why so many questions?"

Ten days, thought Ismail as he gobbled his breakfast of bread and goat's milk. *Ahmadou will never last that long. If Master al-Kabir discovers our trick, he will tell my father for sure.* For the first time, Ismail saw the danger of his game of adventure. *I must get to Ahmadou!*

The Adventure Begins

Ismail followed Ahmadou's father through the market to the camel stables. There, Ibrahim ordered him to hitch the lead camel.

"Bela!" Ismail said gladly. He had made friends with Bela the day before. He would saddle the camel quickly and ride to the palace before the caravan departed.

"No, not Bela," Ibrahim corrected him. "This time, Jos will lead the camel train."

Frantic, Ismail sought out the camel named Jos. "Which one are you?" he asked as he passed the many stalls. He came upon a dark brown male. "Jos?"

The reclining camel snorted. Ismail opened the gate and slowly stepped inside the stall. "I must hitch you up to the camel train, and then I'll hurry off to Ahmadou. Be like a horse. Listen to reason."

It took seven attempts before Ismail secured the saddle over the camel's hump. How had Ahmadou done it so easily? He was finally able to walk the animal onto the open road.

By now, the other animals were waiting in line: eight camels in various shades, heights, and ages; mules carrying Jamilla, Kavitha, Tiye, and the family's possessions; and a lone, skinny goat.

In front of the line, some distance ahead already, Ibrahim sat regally atop his riding camel, Gilda. From behind his veil, he glared at Ismail. "We have lost precious time waiting for you. The sun is already rising. Hitch Jos to the lead quickly. We must go now."

"But …" Ismail began, his heart sinking. How could he leave Timbuktu for a long desert crossing and continue the disguise? He thought of running away, but then he realized that they must all help out if they are to survive. With trembling hands and a twinge of excitement, he hitched Jos to the front of the line. He was going to journey across the desert at last!

The line of camels swayed from side to side as they departed Timbuktu, leaving a line of footprints in the sand.

"Father," Ismail said after a time.

Ibrahim was irritated. "What is it, Ahmadou?"

"Will it really be ten days before we get to Walata?"

Ibrahim took a long time to reply. "The world is full of mystery, Ahmadou, so do not ask me to predict the future. We will get there when we get there. Now, do not disturb the peace of the desert."

"Yes, Father," said Ismail with a sigh.

🐪 🐪 🐪 🐪 🐪 🐪

Ahmadou was so comfortable in Ismail's bed that he was still sleeping soundly long after the rooster's crowing had roused the other scholars.

"Prince Ismail!" Sudi cried. "You are late for school!"

Ahmadou jumped out of the bed. "What? Who?" he called out. He did not recognize anything. Then he remembered where he was and why.

"I have to get back to my family," said Ahmadou.

Sudi eyed him coldly, thinking, *This is no doubt another one of the prince's tricks to get out of school.* "You are a son of a griot. You must learn to write the stories of your ancestors."

Ahmadou answered as if he were Ismail. "I am more interested in what is going on in the marketplace or at the Kabara Port on the river. I have no interest in history."

"You had better not let your father hear you say that," Sudi warned. "Hurry and dress for school."

Ahmadou did what he was told. He did not want to think about the consequences of admitting that he was a poor nomad boy pretending to be Prince Ismail!

Sudi walked the two miles with him to the school. The boy hesitated at the door, afraid to enter the hallowed halls of a Timbuktu academy, even though he had dreamed of doing it so many times before.

Ahmadou was sorry that he had ever agreed to Ismail's game. How would anyone believe he was a prince when he could barely read?

"I will not leave this spot until you are inside!" Sudi called. "I lost track of you yesterday, but today I will be more careful."

"I believe you," Ahmadou sighed and went inside.

Walking gingerly so as not to make a sound, Ahmadou passed several small rooms. The low murmur of teachers' voices drifted into the hallway. He saw groups of boys seated on the ground, their wooden desks and ink stands beside them. He paused before a room of boys who looked to be his own age.

"Excuse me, Master," he interrupted.

Master al-Kabir, a long-faced, white-turbaned old man, turned with a scowl on his face and stared directly at Ahmadou. "How dare you be late for my history class, Ismail! You will stay after school and copy 20 pages. Now, take your seat."

Scrambling to the only empty place, Ahmadou collapsed into a seat. He felt sure the boys could tell he was an impostor, but no one said a word. His stomach was knotted in fear, but he breathed deeply and comforted himself. *At the end of the day, Ismail will return,* he thought. *Tomorrow, everything would go back to the way it was. Until then, I must stay out of trouble.* He bowed his head, hoping everyone would forget about him.

In the Desert

Ismail trudged through the sand at the agonizingly slow pace set by Ahmadou's father's camel. "Why can't the beast walk any faster?" Ismail grumbled to himself. His bare feet stung and burned. He wanted to climb on Jos's saddle, but the camel stared him away.

When Ahmadou's father finally announced, "We will camp here for the night," Ismail's thoughts flew to a soft mat and a bucket of fresh water, but he knew by now that the animals must be cared for first.

Jamilla and the girls immediately began unpacking the mules. Ismail and Ibrahim had to feed and settle the animals. There would be no rest for hours.

"Why should you eat before I do?" the prince grumbled aloud to the mules and goat.

He did not think he could feel more thirsty. The water they carried had to last two more days before they reached a new water source.

"This is why you walk so slowly," Ismail complained. "You conserve water, so you are in no hurry for it."

Ismail's task was to loop the rope around one of Jos's front legs and one of his back legs. Whenever Ismail approached the camel, Jos bucked, kicked, and spat.

Ismail glared at the animal. "You are the source of my trouble."

Finally, Ismail succeeded in looping the rope around one of the camel's front legs. Jos promptly rose and hopped around on three legs, then settled down. That was good enough for Ismail. The boy ran toward the tent and soon forgot about the stubborn animal.

The next morning, Ismail rose even earlier than Ibrahim to harness the camels. He was determined not to walk across the desert today.

He arrived at the place where he had left the camels the night before, but Jos was gone!

He could not cry out, for this would awaken the others. Frantically, he stared out across the dark vista. No movement or sound provided a clue. Finally, he thought to look down at the sand. He saw the single line of three-legged camel tracks.

Ismail followed the tracks, and there lay Jos, asleep. "Jos!" he cried, startling the animal awake. Jos let out a loud, testy growl.

"Oh, why do you have to be so much trouble?" Ismail asked the camel and sank into the sand. *What was I thinking deciding to come to the desert?*

"Bela did her job leading the caravan on the last trip. Now, it is your turn to lead," Ismail said to Jos.

The boy suddenly stopped. *Why am I talking to a camel, as if it could understand me?* he asked himself. He was even more surprised when Jos stirred beside him, as if the camel really could understand him.

"Perhaps you are as unsure about what to do as I am," Ismail said aloud.

"Yaaawwl," the camel said. He nudged Ismail with his huge nose. Then, to Ismail's delight, the bulky camel rocked himself to his feet and stood, waiting.

"We have a lot to learn and another long day ahead of us to learn it, so can we make peace and go back to camp?"

Ismail began walking, and Jos followed.

Ismail constantly felt hungry and tired. When he returned to the camp, he crawled into the tent and collapsed onto his mat.

"Ahmadou, you look ill," Jamilla commented. "What is wrong with you? You don't seem like yourself lately."

This is a chance to confess my disguise, but what good would that do now?

"I am fine, Mother," Ismail replied. "Don't worry about me."

Jamilla, though, was sure that something was different.

As the caravan began the seventh day of the trek, Ismail thought he could bear it no longer. Their water supply was already low, and they would not reach the next watering hole for another day.

The temperature rose to 100 degrees, and a strong wind from the east blew sand in their faces. Ismail pulled his veil over his mouth and his nose. The boy even pulled a thin layer across his eyes. It was through this blue veil that he spotted the beautiful sight. In the distance, glimmering in the sunlight, he saw crystal blue water. He ran to tell his mother.

"Mother, ask Tiye or Kavitha to lead Jos while I go get water from that pond!" Not waiting for a reply, he ran toward the vision.

"Ahmadou, where are you going?" Jamilla called to him, but her voice was carried off in a strong gust of wind.

Ismail kicked up clouds of dust as he ran toward the shimmering water. He did not hear them calling him.

As he ran, he didn't seem to be getting any closer to the pond. Had he misjudged the distance? Before him, the water shimmered with hope of relief. He would dunk his entire head, veil and all, in its cool waves. He would fill the goatskins to the brim and take them to his family. He would be a hero.

However, no matter how much he ran, he could not catch up to the vision. *Of course!* he thought, feeling disappointment so bitter he could taste it. *This is a mirage, a trick of the heated air and the light.* He stopped running and looked back toward the caravan, but he could not see it.

The blowing sand had covered over his footsteps. Ismail turned around several times until the second devastating realization came upon him. He was lost.

Soon after, he heard a rumbling sound in the distance. A low-hanging pale yellow cloud of dust advanced from the east. It was a sandstorm!

For being an hour late, Ahmadou had to remain twice that long after school. He sat under the scornful eye of Master al-Kabir.

The nomad boy, who had never before held a pen, copied the words from the manuscript onto blank sheets of parchment.

He liked filling the pages with beautiful marks. He recognized some of the words, but many words were difficult for him to decipher. Still, he was writing!

When two hours had passed, Master al-Kabir rose, strode over to Ahmadou, and said, "You may stop now. Let me see your work."

Ahmadou held up the pages he had copied. Master al-Kabir's frown deepened. "You have completed only half of what I asked. What do you mean by this disobedience, Ismail?"

Ahmadou could not answer. He had done the best he could.

"I am sending word to your father in Niani about how little his son thinks of his studies. As the son of a revered griot, you should know this passage by heart. You have watched your father perform it many times. Why do you dishonor your father?"

Ahmadou had never seen a griot perform any story from the history of Mali.

In his culture, every man and woman was a storyteller. One did not need a special title or an audience to tell a good story.

Many nights, Ahmadou had listened to his own father tell of their ancestors, nomadic traders who had ruled the desert. He wondered if the stories in manuscripts were anything like his father's tales.

Master al-Kabir shook his head. "What will become of you, Ismail?"

"I will do better," Ahmadou managed.

The exasperated teacher sighed. "Finish the pages tonight. Tomorrow, you will read what you have copied to the class."

"Yes, Master al-Kabir," Ahmadou replied gratefully and fled the building.

He waited at the gated wall a long time, but the prince never returned. Ahmadou ran to his family's tent, but it was gone.

"What happened to Ibrahim, Jamilla, and their three children?" Ahmadou asked a family eating supper in a nearby tent.

A man answered, "Who wants to know?"

The boy started to say, "I am their son," but stopped. Instead, in his princely voice he said, "I am Ismail, Prince of Mali. I command you to answer my question."

The man addressed the boy respectfully. "Son of Mali, Ibrahim and his family departed for Walata before the sun rose. They heard about a prime supply of pure salt, which will bring a big profit in the Timbuktu market. It is a risky time to be on the caravan road, but Ibrahim decided to make one last trip before the season ends and the big sandstorms come."

Ahmadou stared at the man. *How could they go to Walata without me?* he thought. *What will I do?* If Ismail had gone with his family, then he knew he must return to the palace and continue pretending to be Ismail.

"As soon as the family returns, tell them to come to the palace," he commanded the man.

"Yes, oh great son of Mali."

Ahmadou gave the man one of several gold coins that Ismail had left for him, and he walked back to the palace with heavy footsteps.

After the evening meal, Ahmadou copied all of the pages his teacher had given him. At last, he sank into the soft bed cushions in Ismail's room. *Master al-Kabir expects me to read to the class tomorrow,* he thought. *At that time, the truth will surely come to light. Until then, I must continue the game— a game that had started so innocently.*

If my family has taken Ismail with them, they will be back in a day. That pampered prince will not last long in the desert. He will reveal his true identity and command them to return to Timbuktu. When I wake up tomorrow, they will have returned. Ismail will come straight to the palace, and I will not have to go to school. These were Ahmadou's last, hopeful thoughts before his heavy eyelids closed in sleep.

The Rescue

Sand rose and swirled in great gusts. Ismail's robes flapped about wildly, and his veil began to unravel. The pale yellow storm cloud thundered across the sand. "Father!" he cried.

Ibrahim galloped across the blowing sand, following the cry for help. He spotted Ismail in the distance. "Ahmadou!" he called.

"Father!" Ismail repeated.

Ibrahim drew his camel up next to the terrified boy, reached down to pull him onto the saddle, and then they raced away from the storm. Ismail clung to Ibrahim as the yellow cloud increased in intensity. The camel ran faster than Ismail ever thought possible.

They reached a sand dune with only seconds to spare. The sand swirled over their heads. Tent poles were lifted up into the air. The leather covering followed. Clay pots scattered and broke into pieces. The family crouched low to the ground, holding tightly to each other.

After 20 minutes, the storm was over, and it started to rain. They were all safe. However, the winds had carried away their tent. They would have to sleep exposed to the desert.

The black sky sparkled with stars. Ismail lay beneath the sky, feeling sad and guilty. He had endangered his family.

Ibrahim sat next to Ismail. His expression was unreadable behind his veil.

"Ahmadou, some of my friends think you are too young to wear a veil."

Perhaps now, Ismail thought, *I will tell Ibrahim that I am an impostor.*

"I do not believe this," Ibrahim continued. "You proved yourself on our last trip, but something distracts you now. Is it the lure of words and writing? Would you rather follow a different path?"

How perceptive Ahmadou's father was. His own father would never ask such a question.

"I am sorry, Father, for my mistakes. Please do not lose confidence in me. I will do better."

Ibrahim sighed. He pulled the veil away from his nose and kissed his son's forehead. Then he stood up to leave. "We must spend some of our salt profits on a new tent and supplies. I think there will be enough money that we can send you to school in Timbuktu until the next caravan season."

"Thank you, Father," Ismail said. *First*, he thought, *I'll have to tell my father everything.*

No miracle happened overnight. Ismail did not return. With a sense of dread, Ahmadou prepared for his second day of school. He had copied page after page of words, but he wasn't sure what many of the words said or how he would be able to read them.

With his head down, Ahmadou walked with the other boys to school. "Ismail, is your right hand aching from all that copying? Do you have blisters, like a nomad boy?" a boy teased. As Ahmadou drew his hands behind him, his anger simmered, for he was proud of what his family did.

"What do you mean?" Ahmadou demanded.

"You know what those nomads we see in the street are like," said one of the boys, "all dusty and tattered. They even smell like their precious camels!"

Ahmadou charged at the boy. As the two tussled back and forth in the sand, Ahmadou dropped his bag, and the pages he had copied spilled out. Ahmadou had strong muscles and hurt pride, so within a minute, he had pinned his opponent to the ground. The boy gave in and apologized.

"My pages!" Ahmadou exclaimed as a wind blew them. "Help me gather them, please!" The two boys ran about frantically. When the last page had been collected, the boys laughed with relief.

Ahmadou got an idea. He turned to the boy. "You apologized, but I demand payment. Here!" He thrust the papers at the boy. "You must read these pages aloud before we reach school. Then I will forgive you."

That is how Ahmadou read to Master al-Kabir in class that day.

As the days passed, Ahmadou began to enjoy the life of a prince. He was never hungry or cold. He had no physical labor to do; studying was his only work. He found other students willing to read aloud to him, and he began to understand the words. He was drawn to the very stories about past rulers and soldiers that had so wearied Ismail. After he had completed his lessons, he would burn the candle down to the wick, writing page after page, even after his hand would cramp.

He wrote down the stories of his people. These were the stories told by his father around desert campfires on cool, windy nights. He knew them by heart.

"Never forget, children," Ibrahim would always begin, "that you are descended from generations of blue-veiled men of the desert, expert cameleers and traders. Nomads founded the city of Timbuktu."

"Tell us the story, Father," Ahmadou, Kavitha, and Tiye would say, their eyes bright and eager in the firelight.

Ibrahim would recite, "One day, the traders left all of their supplies at a watering hole in the Sahel. They left these in the care of a nomad woman named Bouctou. When the men returned, they decided to make a permanent town there. They named it in honor of the woman who had taken such great care of their property. The place became *tim bouctou*, the place belonging to Bouctou. That was the beginning of the Bright City."

Ahmadou thrived in school, but as time passed, another trouble arose: Botu's upcoming wedding. *If my family has made it safely to Walata and are on their way back, they should arrive any day now and bring Ismail back,* he told himself.

When there were only two days left before the wedding, Ahmadou went to Botu's room. "Botu," he said, "tell me again what I must do at your wedding."

"Nothing less than ensure the longevity and prosperity of my marriage!" the older prince exclaimed. "That is something you alone, being my only brother, can do." The groom-to-be explained that after the bride's Songhai family had presented all of their gifts to the groom's Malian family at the wedding, Ismail was to "capture" Princess Amina. He was to carry her before her future husband and then sing Botu's praises, as a griot does for a king.

"You know me better than anyone, Ismail. You must convince Princess Amina of all my good qualities so that she will consent to marry me. It is tradition. If my brother does not do this well, I will live as a miserable husband!"

Ahmadou sighed deeply. He wondered, *Will I have to pretend to be Prince Ismail for the rest of my life?*

The Wedding

All of Timbuktu turned out for Botu's wedding. Women wore brightly colored garments and matching wraps, their beaded necklaces jingling as they walked. The men walked about in their best robes.

Ahmadou scanned the crowd nervously for his parents. He stood beside Botu on a raised platform, both boys dressed in silken robes and ruby-studded turbans. Ismail's father, Mohammed el-Bekri, presided over the festivities, while Ismail's mother smiled and made everyone welcome. The women of the court sat in a circle. Palace guards wore bright red tunics and held swords with gold handles.

Mohammed el-Bekri had not said much to the boy he thought was Ismail. "Good morning," the father had said in his booming voice. "I hear you are doing well in your studies, Ismail. This is expected of my son."

"Yes, Father," Ahmadou had replied. Then, he kept as far away from him as he could.

The ceremony began when the palace drummers announced the arrival of the Songhai family. The bride's father and the royal entourage marched toward the platform. The father summoned servant after servant, bearing gifts of gold boxes, jewelry, statues, and musical instruments.

Songhai dancers entered in a rush of scarlet, blue, and purple feathers. They formed five rows of ten dancers, yet they moved as one. Their feet pounded the same rhythm, and their arms cut the same wide arcs in the air.

When the performance ended, no one moved. Then came a great clamor of cheers. Ahmadou braced himself. It was time for him to capture the princess—but suddenly, a voice broke through the noise.

"Stop!" the voice called out. "This wedding must not continue. Prince Ismail is an impostor. I am the real prince!"

Cheers dissolved into a collective gasp. A thin, blue-veiled boy made his way along the rows of dancers toward the platform.

Mohammed el-Bekri stood up, outraged. "What is the meaning of this? Seize him!"

Ahmadou could not move, for he could not believe what he was seeing. The guards caught the boy and led him to Mohammed el-Bekri.

"Who are you?" the griot demanded.

Ibrahim and Jamilla broke through the crowd and hurried to Ismail's side. This brought Ahmadou out of his trance. His mother and father were here!

"We are his parents," Ibrahim said to Mohammed, pointing to Ismail. Then, to the boy he said, "Ahmadou, what has gotten into you?"

"Please forgive him, gracious sir," Jamilla said quickly, trying to grab her son from the guard. "We are simple nomads, and we just arrived from a journey across the desert. I think the sun has gotten to him."

"No!" cried Ismail. "I am fine, but I am not her son. I am yours!" He pointed his finger at his father.

"It is my son's wedding day, and I will not punish your son for his foolishness. Take him home," the griot said to Ibrahim.

"No!" said Ahmadou as he stepped forward on the platform.

"This boy is telling the truth," Ahmadou said loudly. "I am a nomad."

The crowd erupted in confusion. The bride's family looked questioningly at each other, and Botu fumed over the interruption. "Ismail! Come to your senses," he hissed. "Let them take this mad boy away, and we will continue the ceremony!"

Ahmadou hurried to Ismail's side. "You see, we traded places," Ahmadou began.

"It was just a prank, Father," Ismail added.

"We found we could fool Botu and my family," Ahmadou continued.

"Then I had to leave suddenly on a desert journey with the nomads . . ." said Ismail.

"Halt!" the griot roared. "This is madness. My son has lost his wits, and so, I fear, has your boy," he said to Jamilla and Ibrahim.

Ahmadou thought quickly. He turned to Sudi. "Go to my room and retrieve the tablets I was writing on the other day. This will prove I am the nomads' son."

Sudi looked for approval from Mohammed el-Bekri. The griot nodded, and Sudi left the courtyard. The two boys looked at each other with a mixture of relief and dismay.

Finally, Sudi returned carrying the tablets. He handed them to Mohammed el-Bekri. He read a few and then gave them to Ahmadou.

"Oh," said Ismail, "he cannot read or write. Give them to me!"

Ahmadou took hold of his pages and proudly proclaimed, "I wrote this with my own hand, and I will read it."

From the first words, Jamilla and Ibrahim looked on in amazement. They were listening to the same tale of his ancestors that Ibrahim had told in the desert.

"My son," Ibrahim said in wonder. "You are my son, for nobody else could have written those words. Yet, how could you have learned to read and write?"

"I have spent nearly the past month in a fine school."

Mohammed el-Bekri still was not convinced. "The two of you look so much alike that it is hard to believe. How can I know who my son is?"

Ismail thought a moment. He ran from the compound and returned, carrying the princess.

"Look, Botu! I have brought you your intended. Now, I will tell her all about you and convince her to be your wife."

When he finished, the crowd burst into cheers. "A splendid griot's performance!" people murmured.

"You see, Father, I am your own son, Ismail. I have survived a long desert journey and have learned much living as a nomad, but I still remember what it means to be the son of a griot."

The griot did not move for a long time. Everyone waited silently. Finally, Mohammed el-Bekri sighed deeply and said, "Ismail, my son, welcome home."

A joyous reunion followed as each boy was embraced by his family. The wedding continued, and the festivities went on for hours. It would have been difficult to say who was happier: The newly married couple or the boys, Ismail and Ahmadou, who were finally back where they belonged.